easy piano **WORSHIP** TO GETHER®

HERE I AM to WORSHIP for kids

ISBN 0-634-09877-2

HAL•LEONARD®
CORPORATION
7777 W. BLUEMOUND RD. P.O. BOX 13819 MILWAUKEE, WI 53213

Visit Hal Leonard Online at
www.halleonard.com

Contents

ABOVE ALL

Words and Music by PAUL BALOCHE
and LENNY LeBLANC

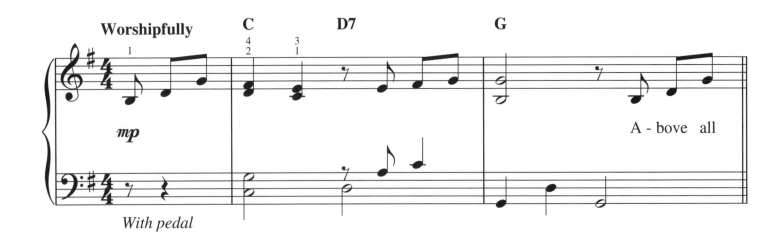

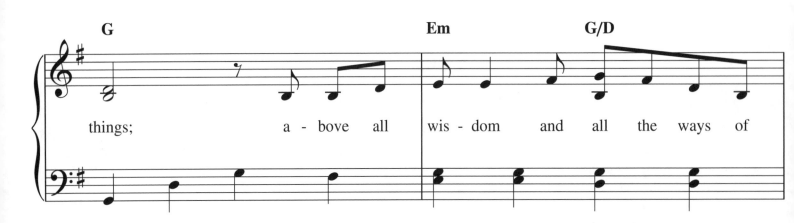

AWESOME GOD
(Your Voice)

Words and Music by
VICKY BEECHING

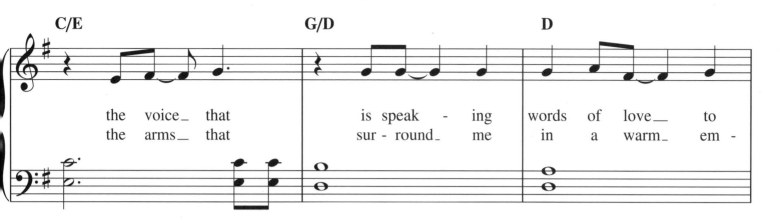

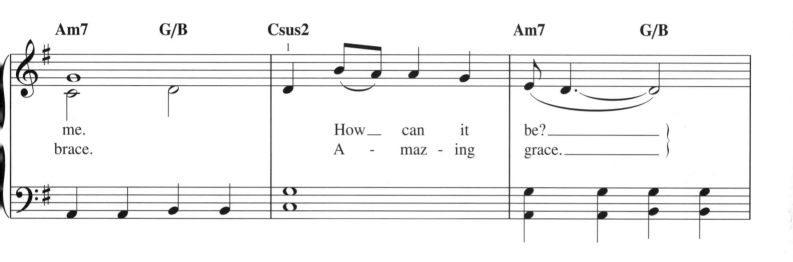

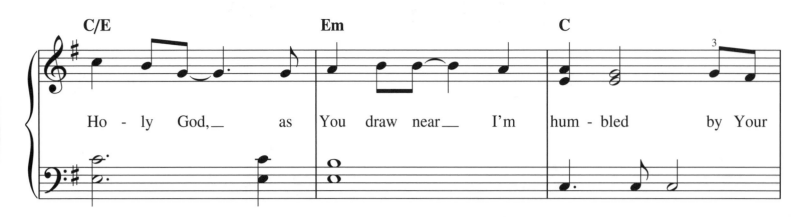

Ho - ly God,___ as You draw near___ I'm hum - bled by Your

maj - es - ty___ and the mys - ter - y___ of

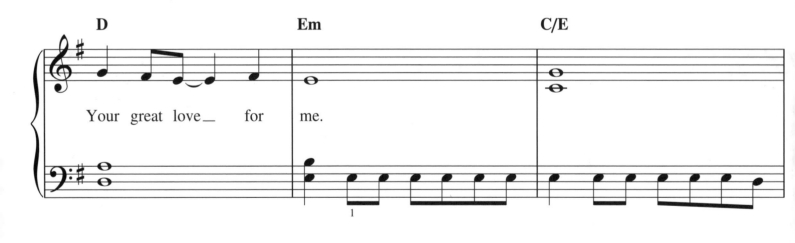

Your great love___ for me.

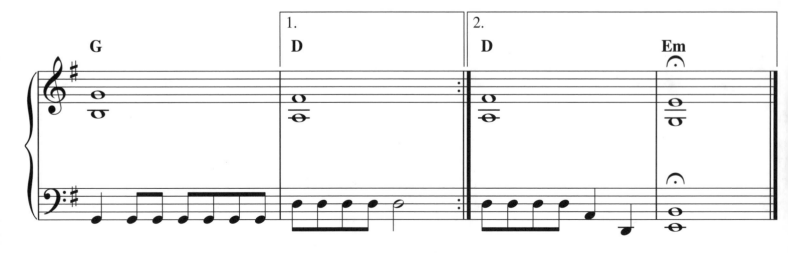

BETTER IS ONE DAY

Words and Music by
MATT REDMAN

else - where._____ Bet - ter is one day in Your courts, bet - ter is

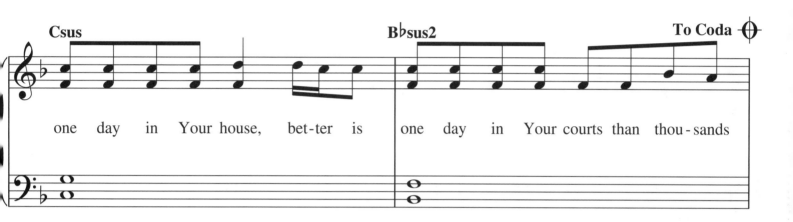

one day in Your house, bet-ter is one day in Your courts than thou-sands

1.
else - where,_____ than thou-sands else - where._ One

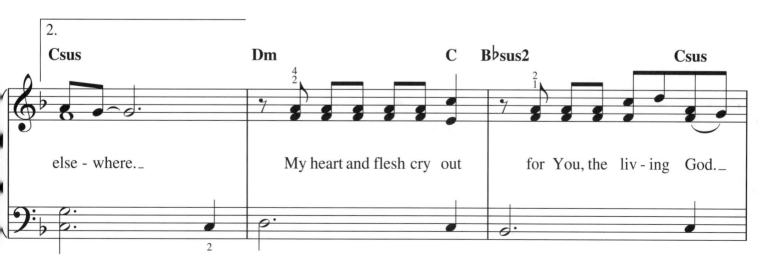

2.
else - where._ My heart and flesh cry out for You, the liv - ing God._

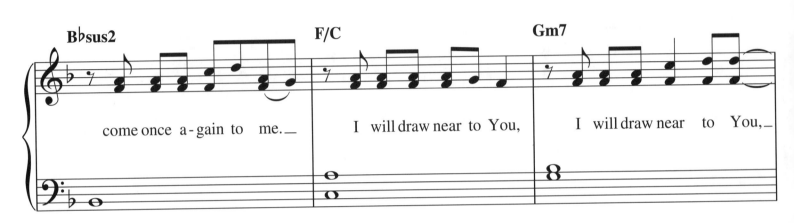

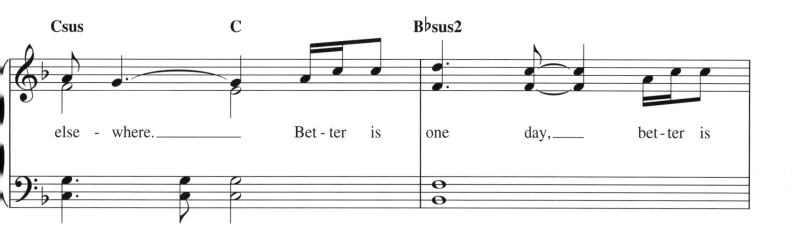

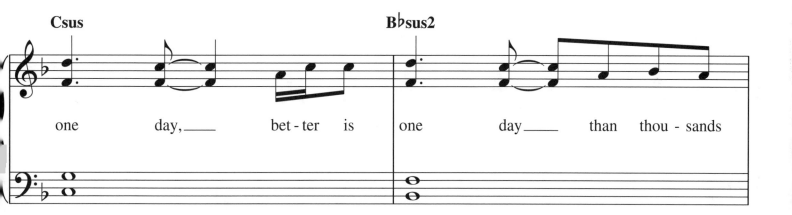

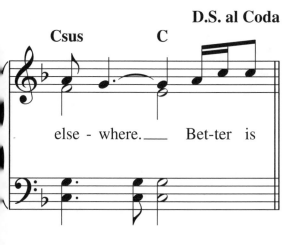

BLESSED BE YOUR NAME

Words and Music by MATT REDMAN
and BETH REDMAN

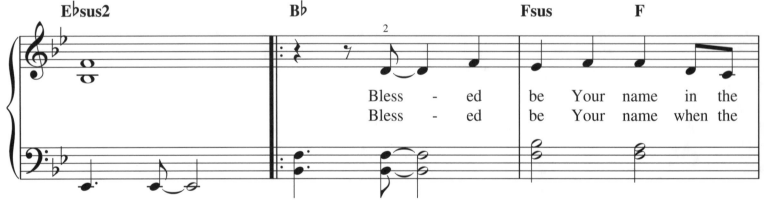

Bless - ed be Your name in the
Bless - ed be Your name when the

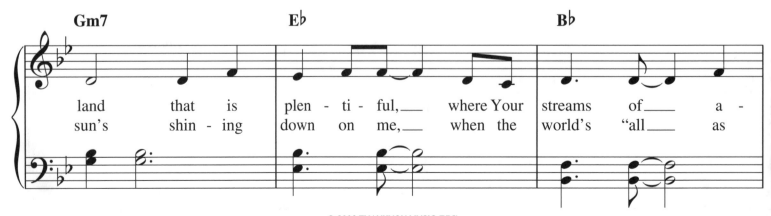

land that is plen - ti - ful,___ where Your streams of___ a -
sun's shin - ing down on me,___ when the world's "all___ as

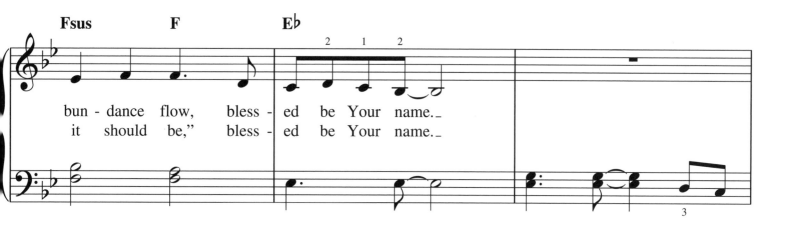

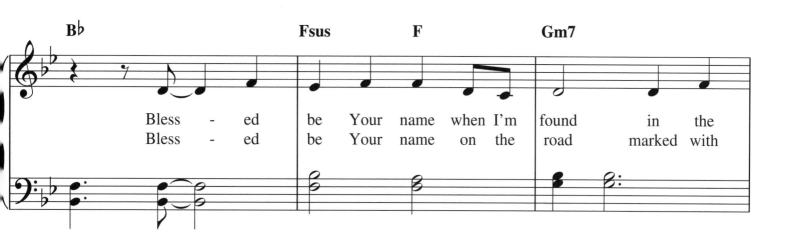

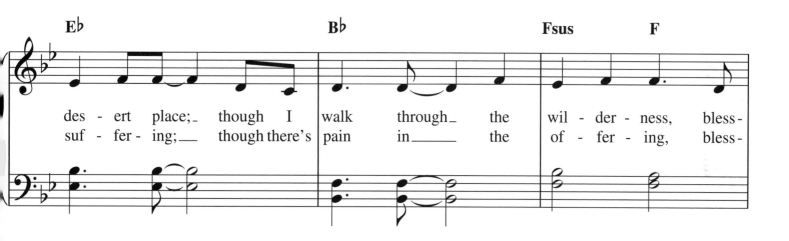

18

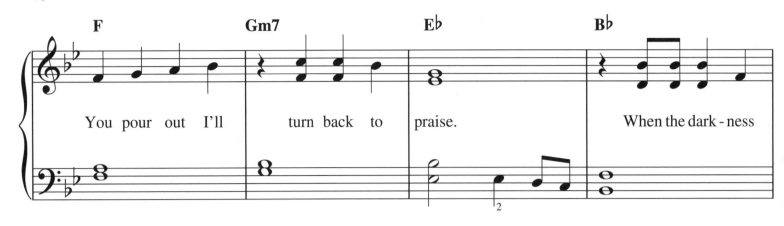

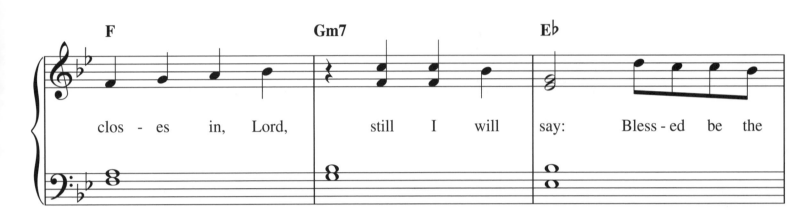

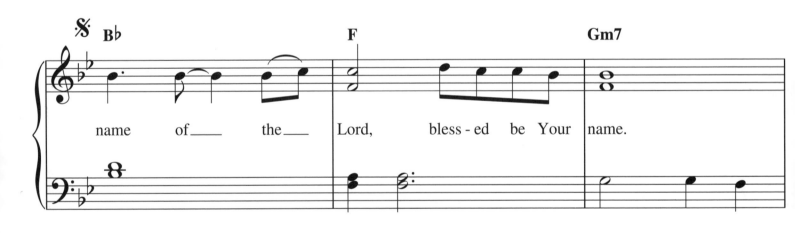

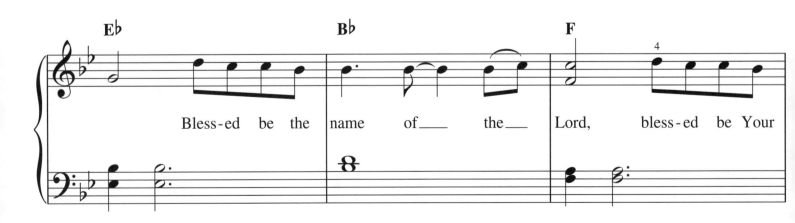

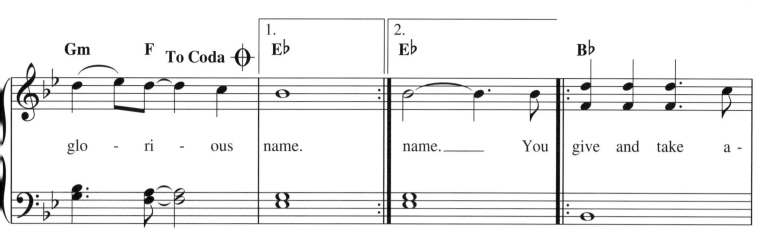

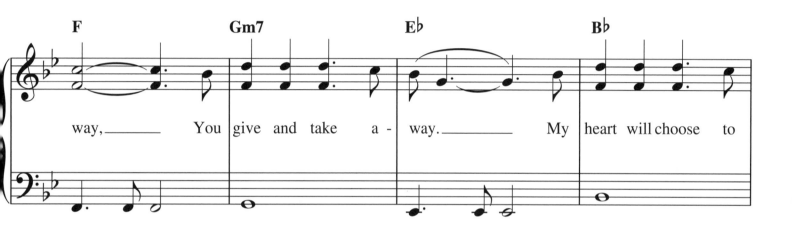

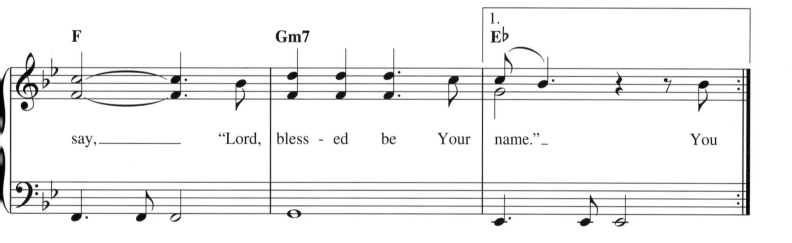

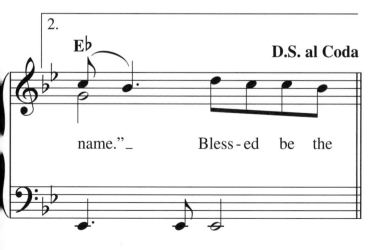

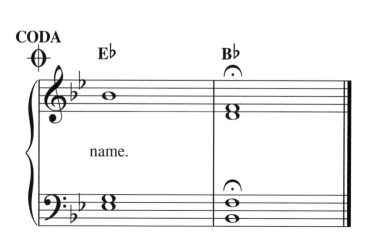

BREATHE

Words and Music by
MARIE BARNETT

FAMOUS ONE

Words and Music by CHRIS TOMLIN
and JESSE REEVES

With excitement

You_____ are the Lord,_____ the

fa - mous One,   fa - mous One.   Great_____ is Your

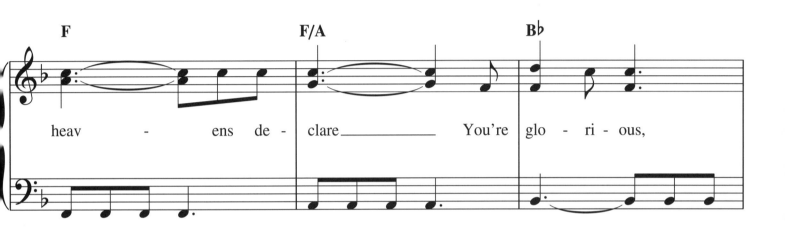

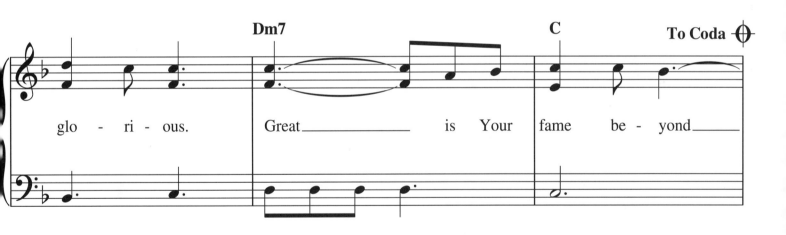

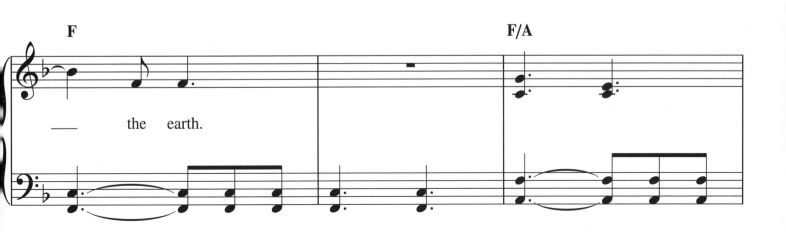

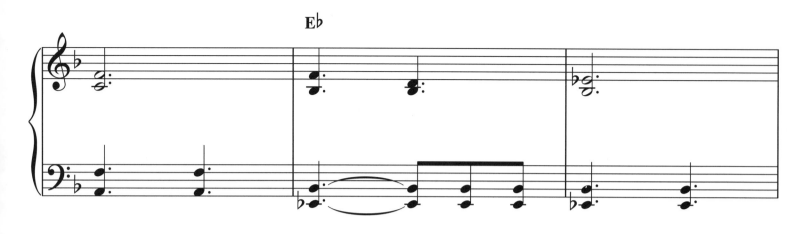

Eb

Bbsus2   Gm7

For all You've
The Morn - ing

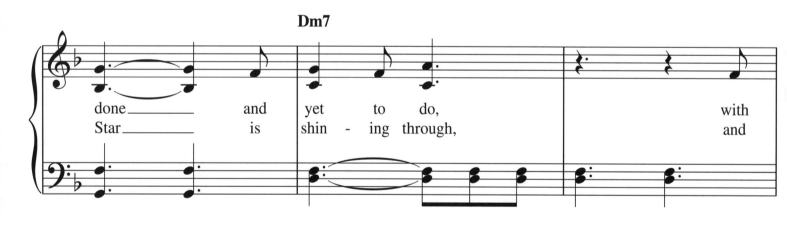

Dm7

done_____ and yet to do,   with
Star_____ is shin - ing through,   and

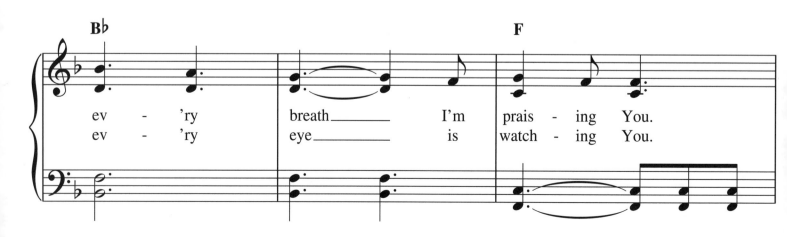

Bb   F

ev - 'ry breath_____ I'm prais - ing You.
ev - 'ry eye_____ is watch - ing You.

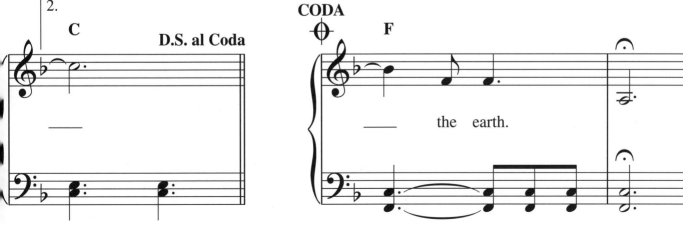

FILLED WITH YOUR GLORY

Words and Music by TIM NEUFELD
and JON NEUFELD

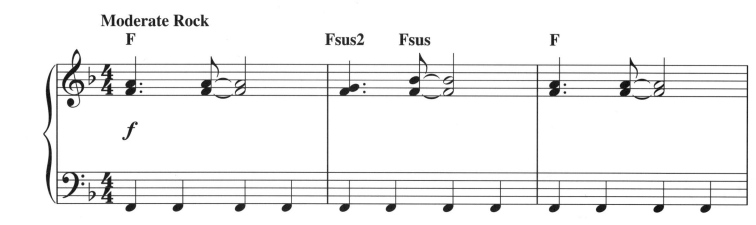

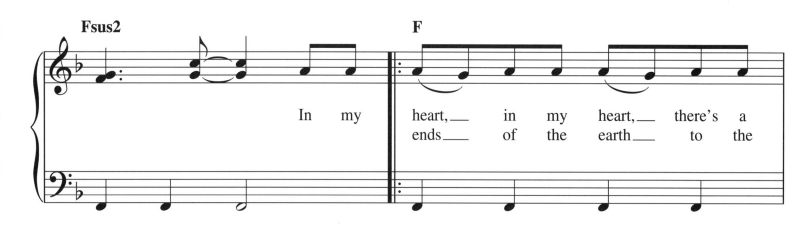

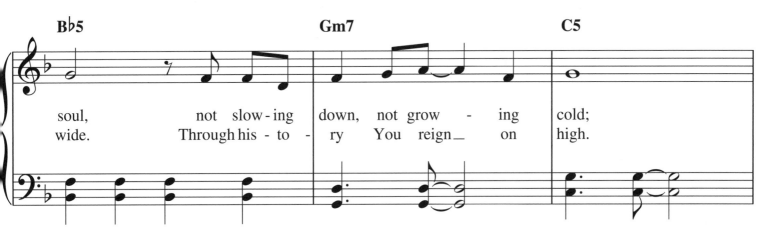

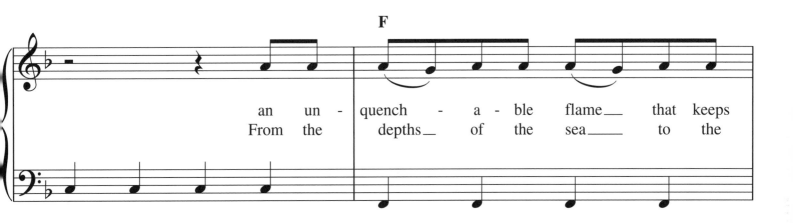

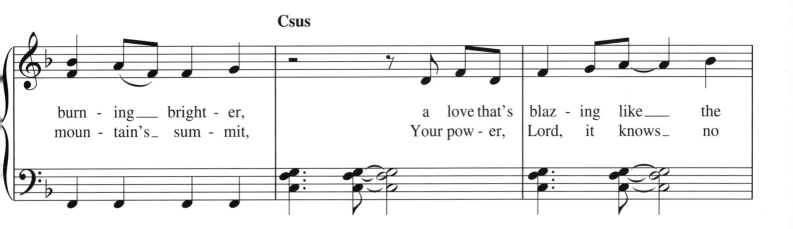

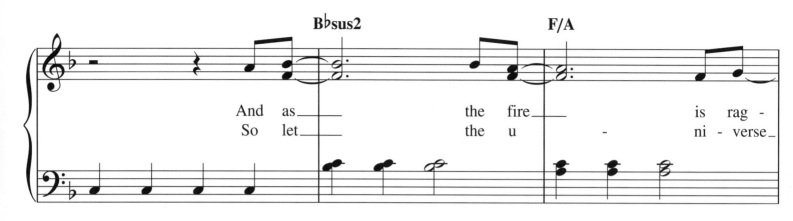

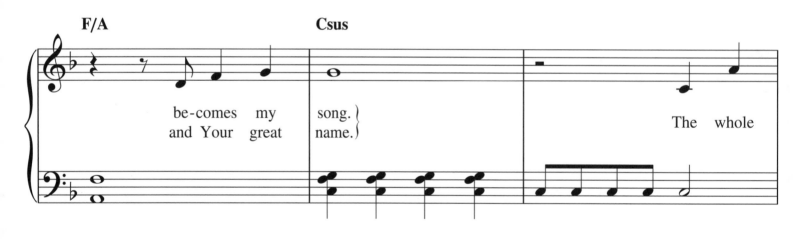

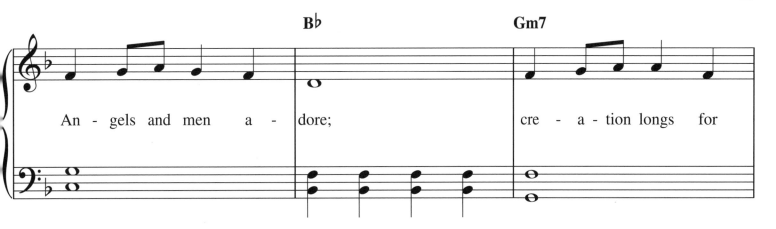

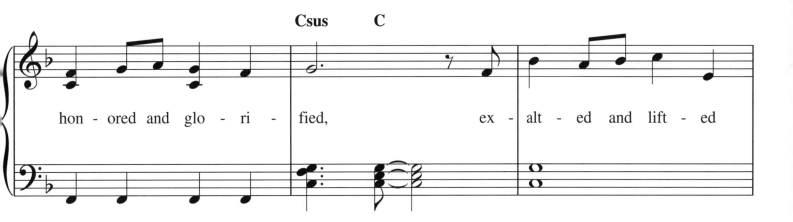

30

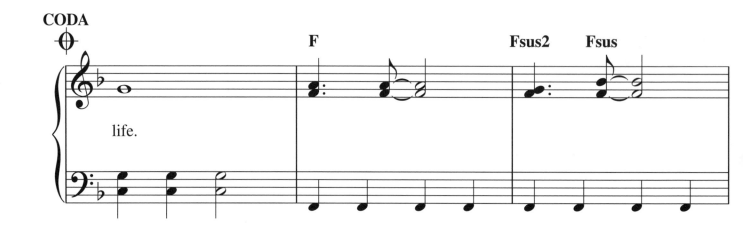

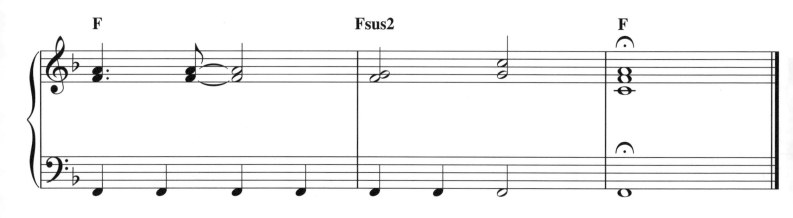

GOD OF WONDERS

Words and Music by MARC BYRD
and STEVE HINDALONG

Moderately, in 2

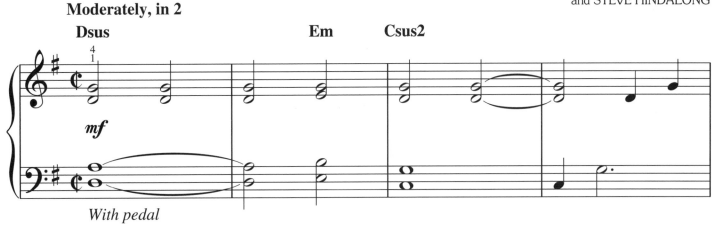

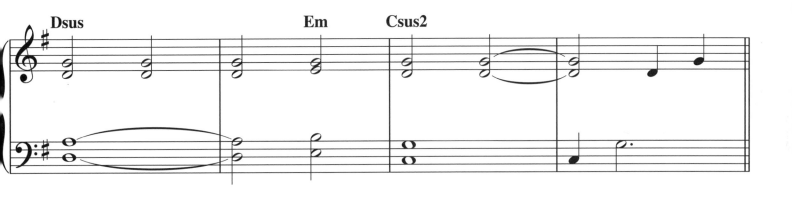

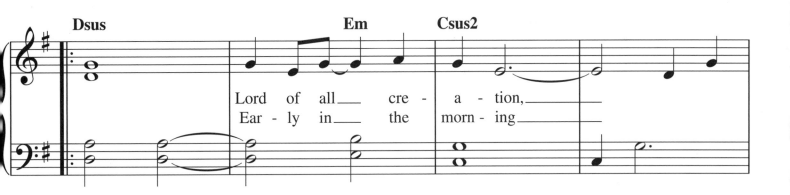

Lord of all____ cre - a - tion,____
Ear - ly in____ the morn - ing____

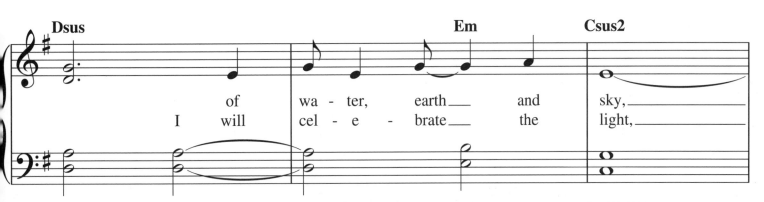

    of   wa - ter, earth____ and   sky,____
I will cel - e - brate____ the light,____

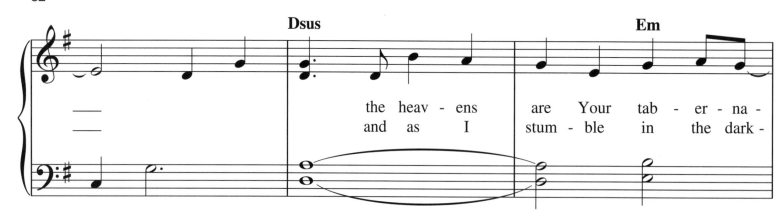

the heav - ens are Your tab - er - na -
and as I stum - ble in the dark -

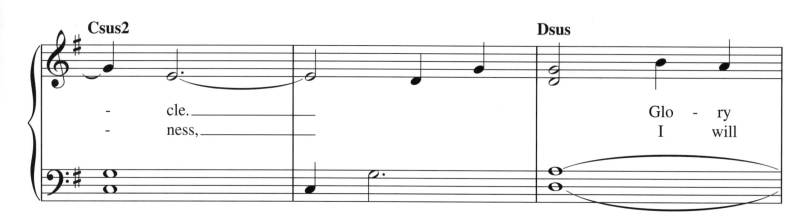

- cle._____
- ness,_____

Glo - ry
I will

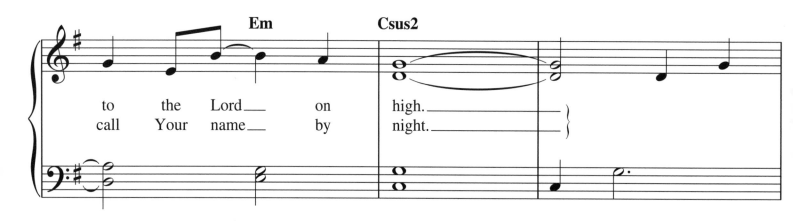

to the Lord___ on high._____
call Your name___ by night._____

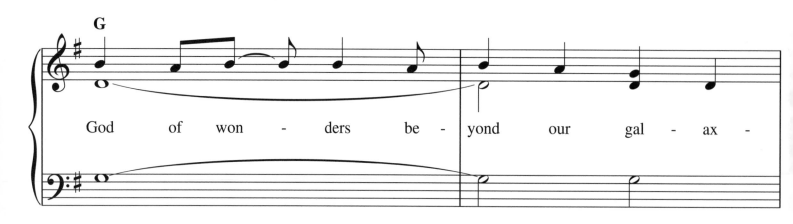

God of won - ders be - yond our gal - ax -

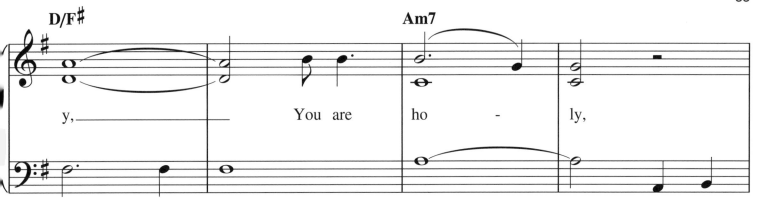

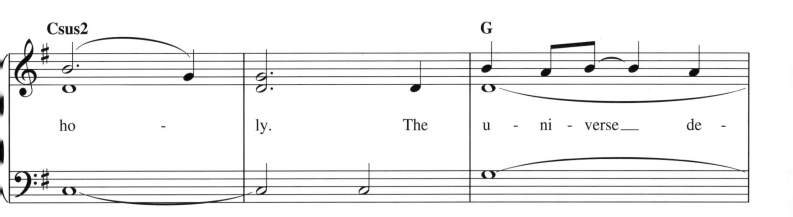

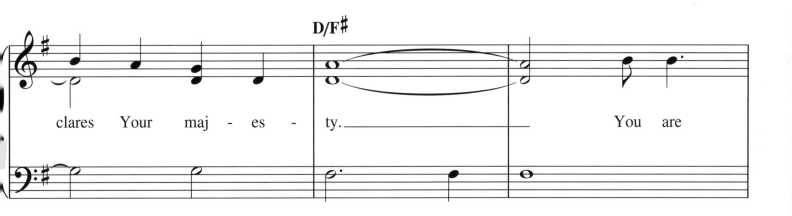

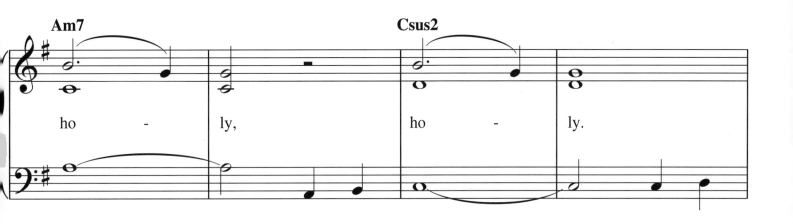

Lord of heav - en and earth,

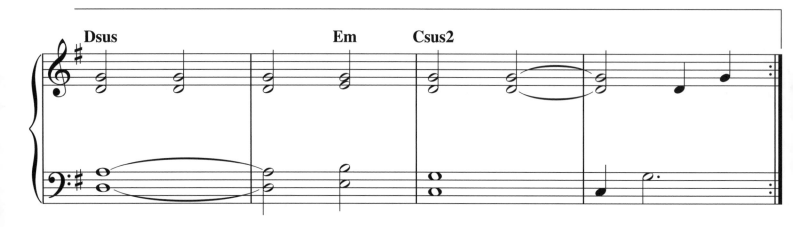

1.

Lord of heav - en and earth.

Dsus   Em   Csus2

2.

G/B   Am7

Hal - le - lu -

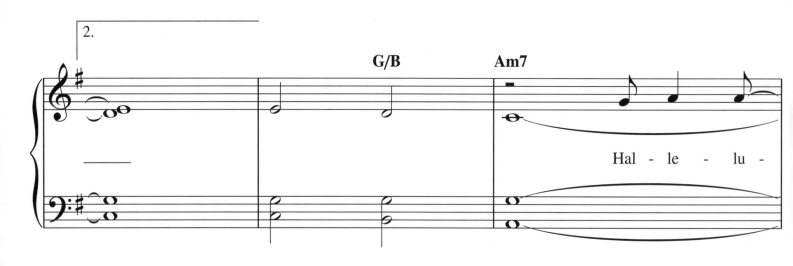

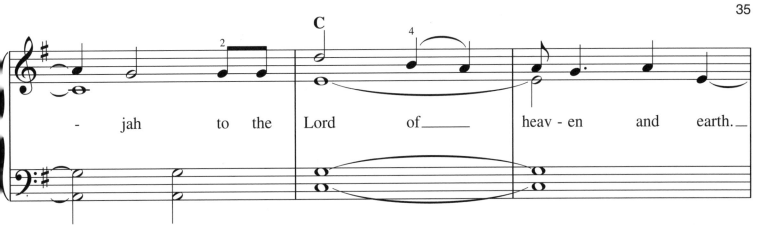

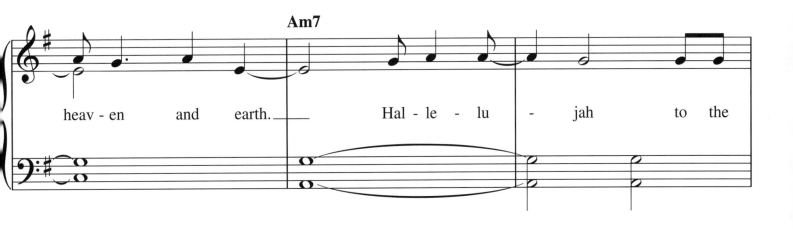

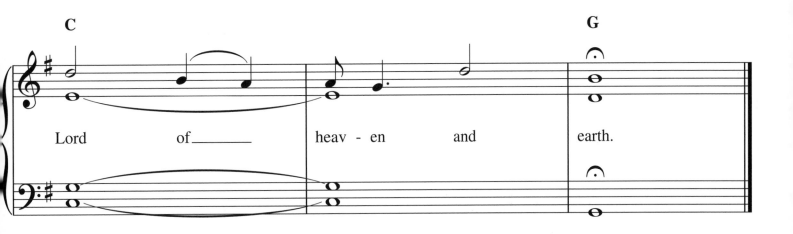

HE IS EXALTED

Words and Music by
TWILA PARIS

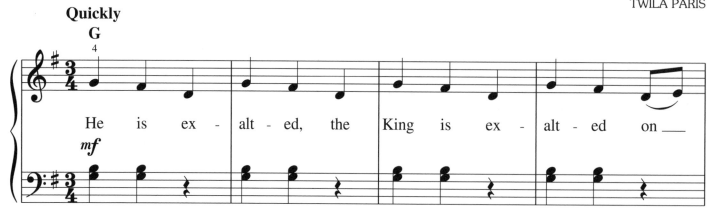

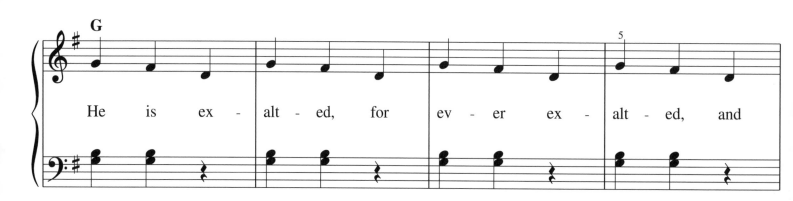

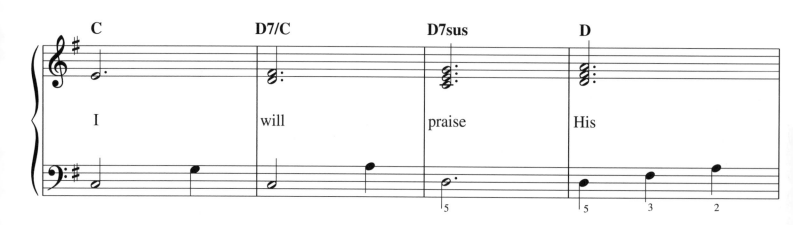

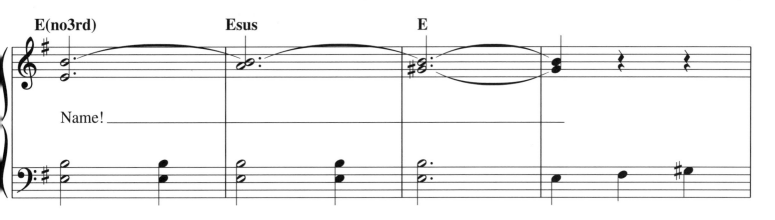

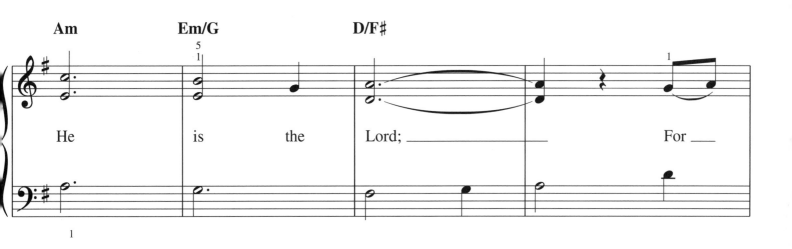

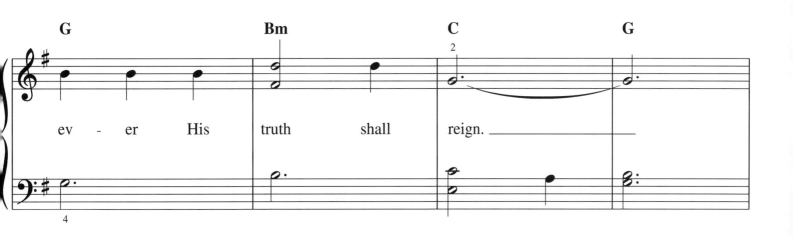

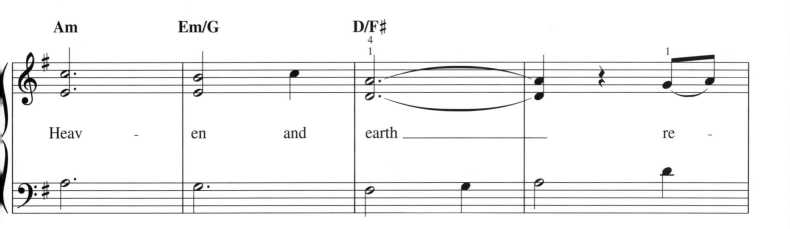

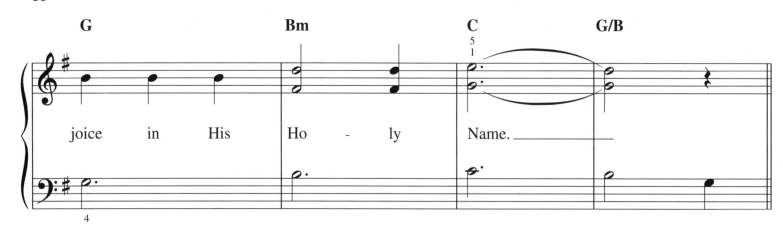

G   Bm   C   G/B

joice in His Ho - ly Name. _____

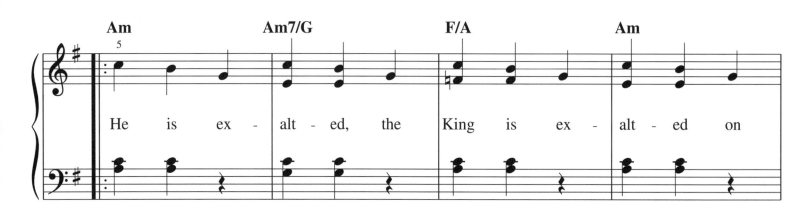

Am   Am7/G   F/A   Am

He is ex - alt - ed, the King is ex - alt - ed on

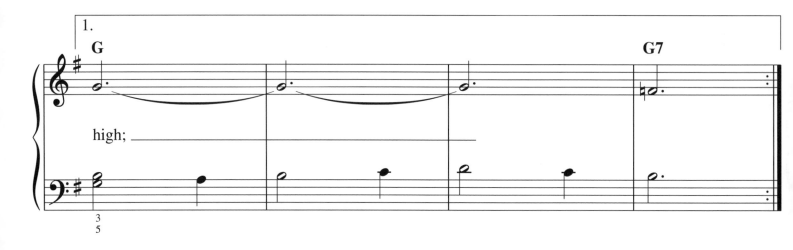

1.

G   G7

high; _____

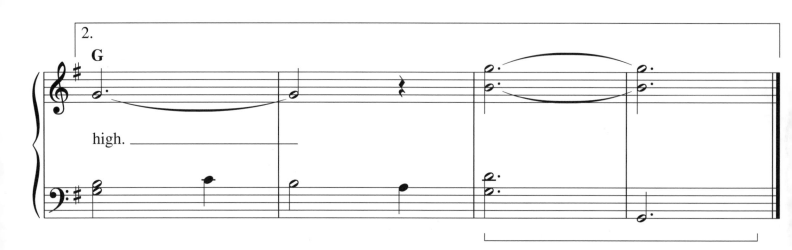

2.

G

high. _____

THE HEART OF WORSHIP

Words and Music by
MATT REDMAN

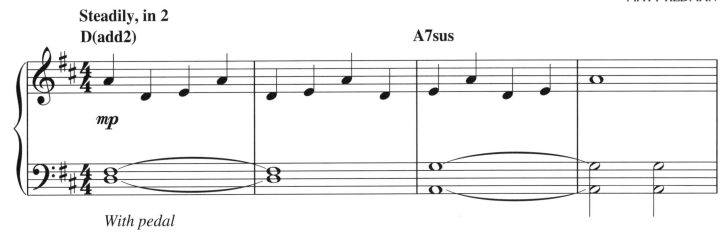

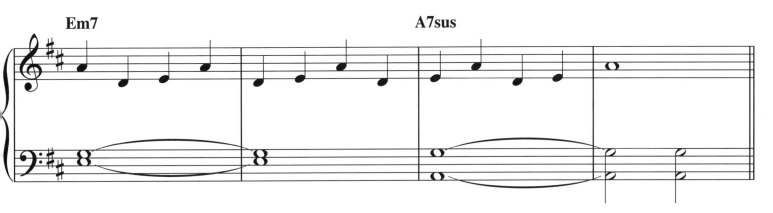

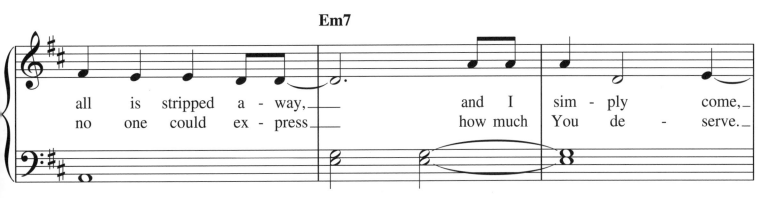

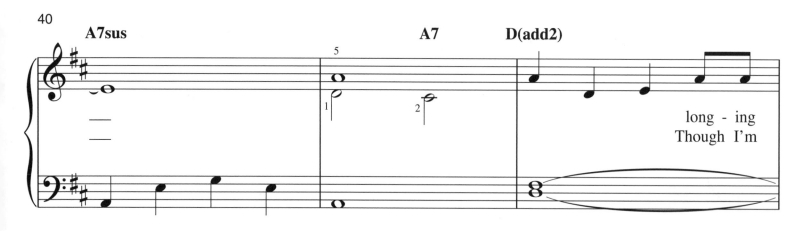

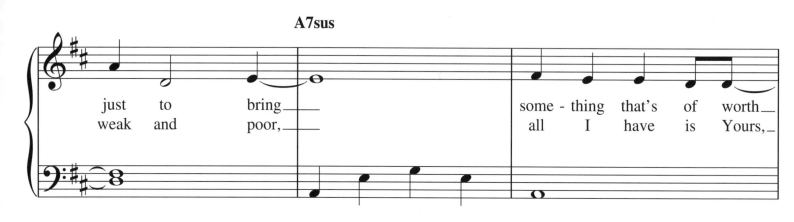

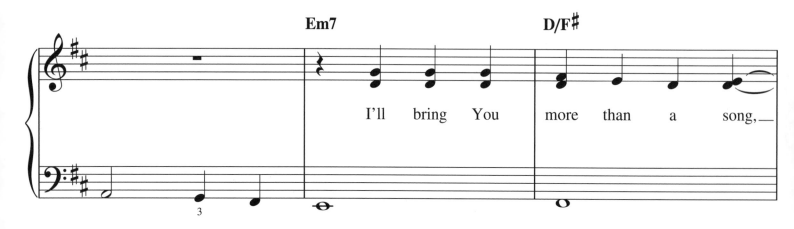

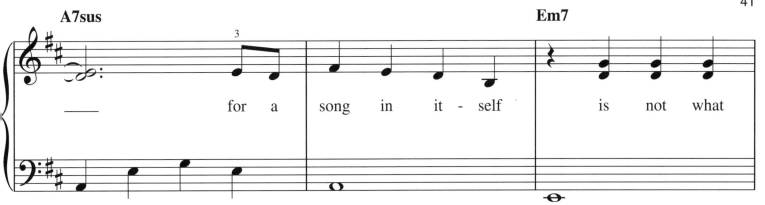

for a song in it - self   is   not   what

You have re - quired.____   You search much

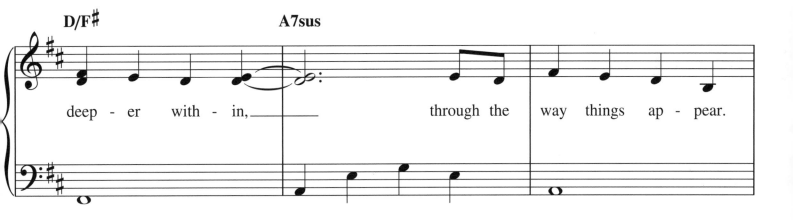

deep - er with - in,____   through the   way things ap - pear.

You're look - ing   in - to   my   heart.____

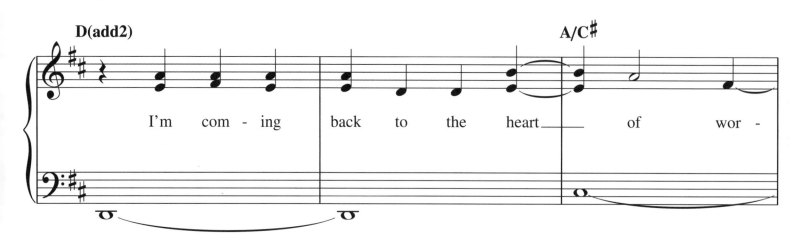

I'm com - ing back to the heart___ of wor -

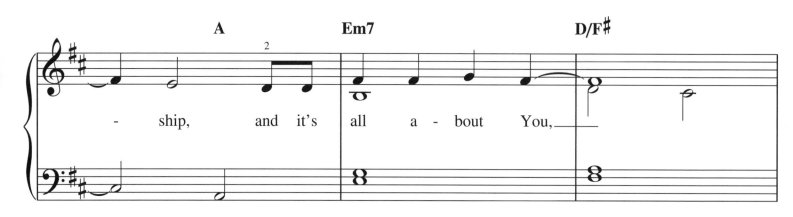

- ship, and it's all a - bout You,___

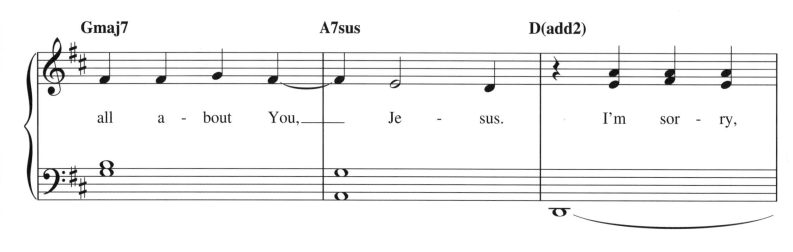

all a - bout You,___ Je - sus. I'm sor - ry,

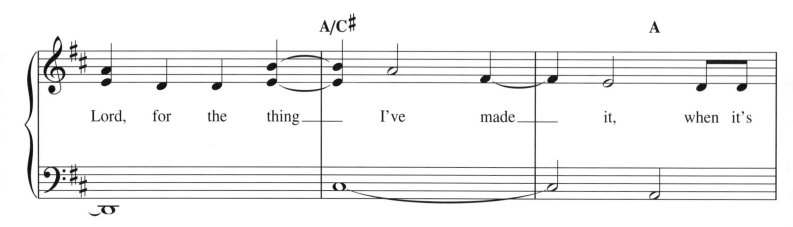

Lord, for the thing___ I've made___ it, when it's

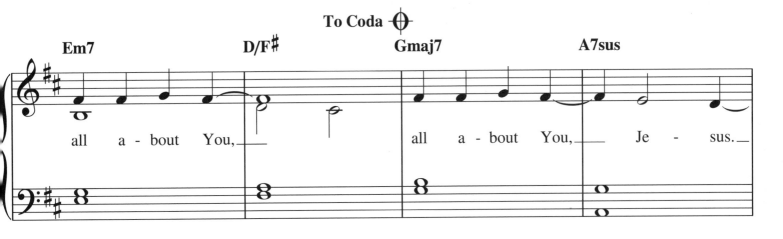

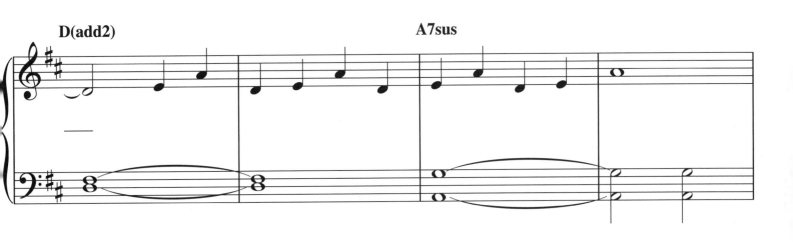

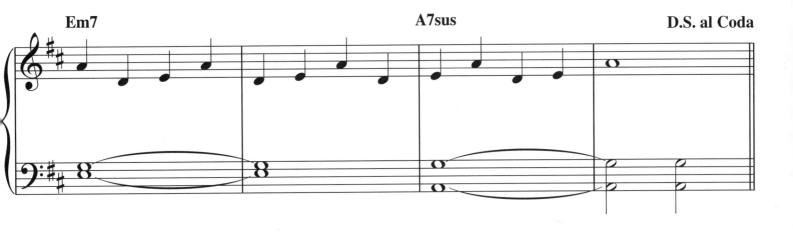

HE REIGNS

Words and Music by PETER FURLER
and STEVE TAYLOR

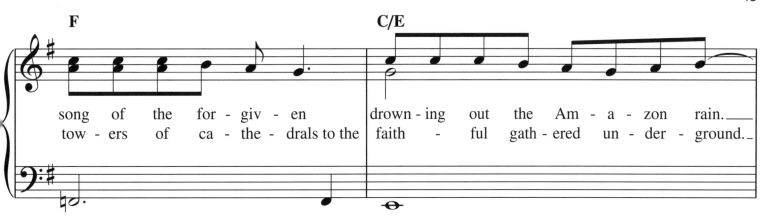

song of the for - giv - en
tow - ers of ca - the - drals to the

drown - ing out the Am - a - zon rain.
faith - ful gath - ered un - der - ground.

The song of
Of all the songs sung from the

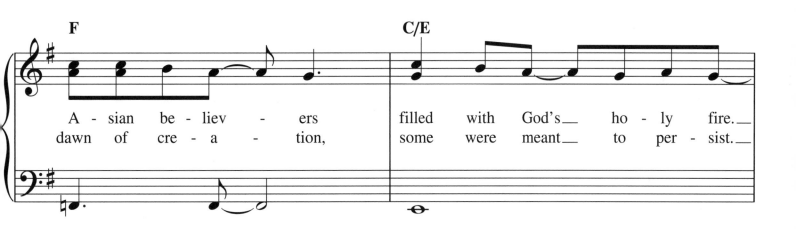

A - sian be - liev - ers
dawn of cre - a - tion,

filled with God's ho - ly fire.
some were meant to per - sist.

It's ev - 'ry tribe, ev - 'ry
Of all the bells rung from a

46

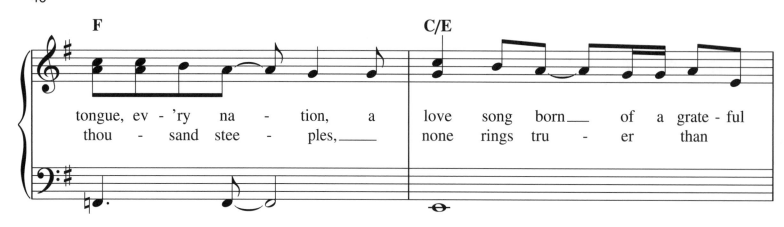

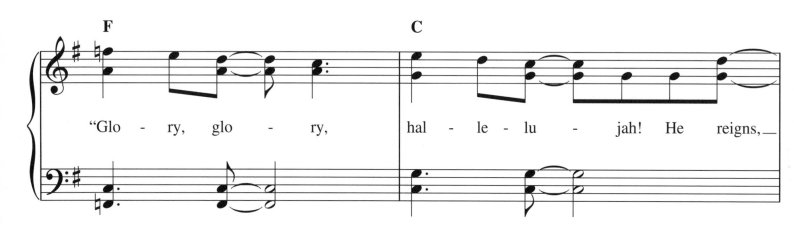

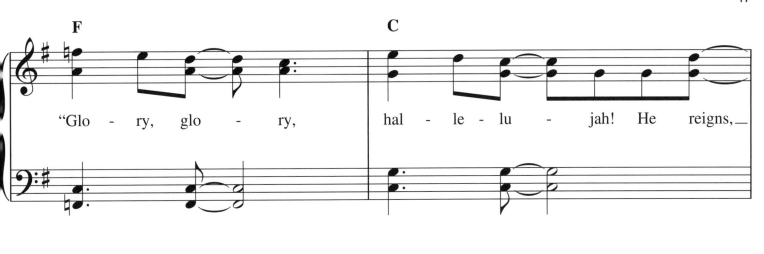

"Glo - ry, glo - ry, hal - le - lu - jah! He reigns,___

___ He reigns!" Let it And all the

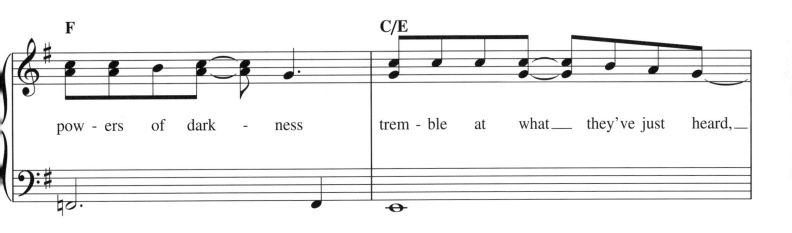

pow - ers of dark - ness trem - ble at what___ they've just heard,___

___ 'cause all the pow - ers of dark - ness

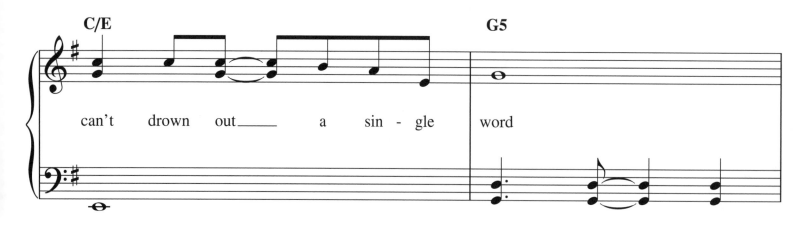

49

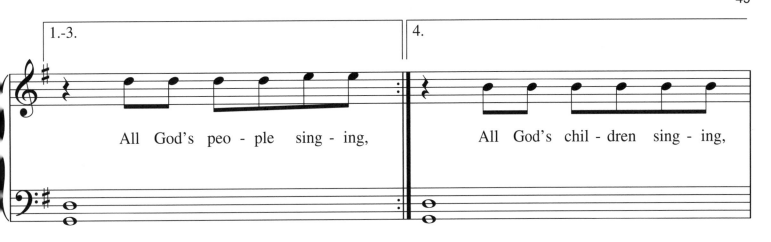

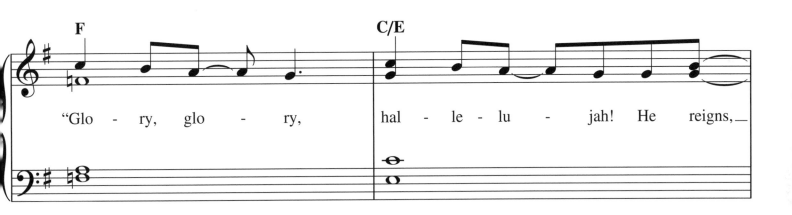

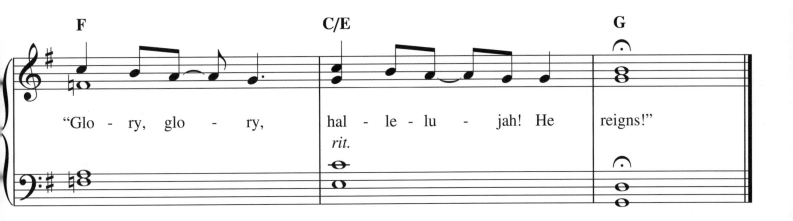

NO ONE LIKE YOU

Words and Music by JACK PARKER,
MIKE DODSON, JASON SOLLEY, MIKE HOGAN,
JEREMY BUSH and DAVID CROWDER

Moderate Rock

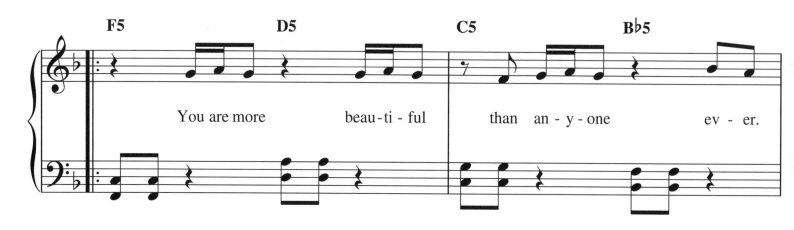

You are more beau-ti-ful than an-y-one ev-er.

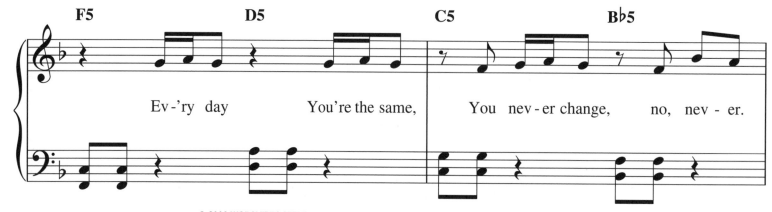

Ev-'ry day You're the same, You nev-er change, no, nev-er.

There is no one like You. There has nev - er,

ev - er been an - y - one like You. You! You! You! You!

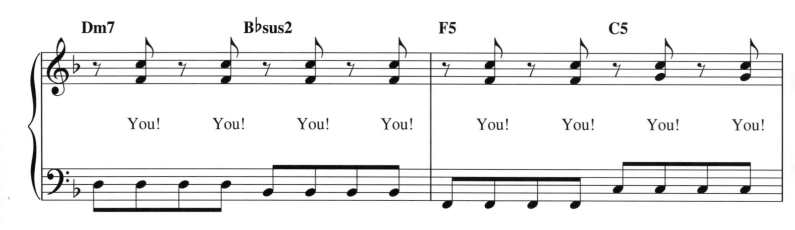

You! You! You! You! You! You! You! You!

You! You! You! You! How could You be so good to

me? How could You be so good to me? How could You

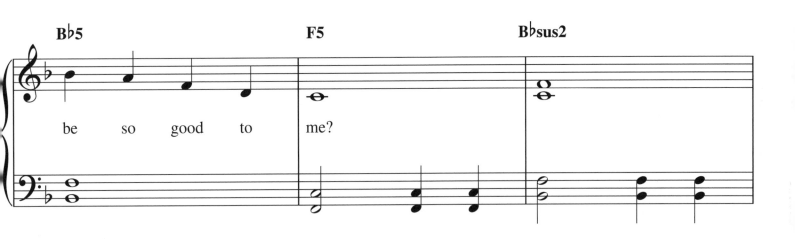

be so good to me?

We're not a - lone,＿ so sing a - long.＿

We're not a - lone,＿ so sing a - long,＿

N.C.

D.S. al Coda

sing a - long,___ sing a - long.___   Here we go!

CODA

Dm   Bb5

ev - er been an - y - one like our God. There is no one,

there is no one like our God. There is no one,

Bbsus2

there is no one like our God.

HERE I AM TO WORSHIP

Words and Music by
TIM HUGHES

Moderately slow

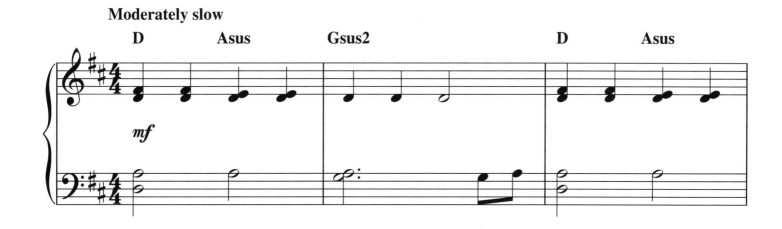

Light of the World, You stepped down in-to dark - ness,
King of all days, oh so high - ly ex - al - ted,

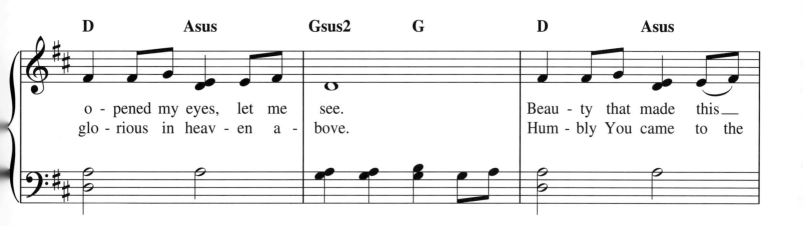

o - pened my eyes, let me see.
glo - rious in heav - en a - bove.

Beau - ty that made this__
Hum - bly You came to the

58

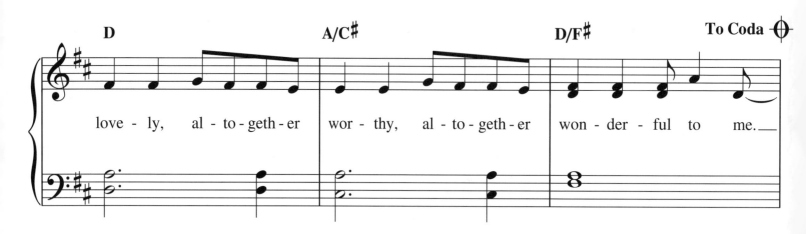

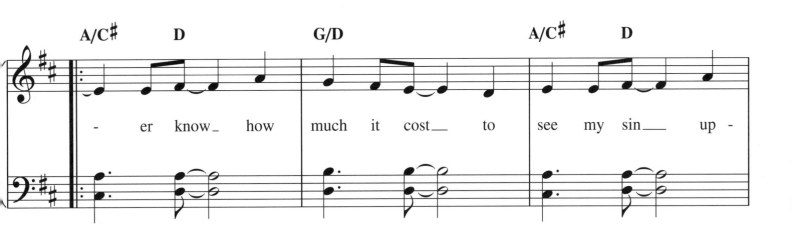

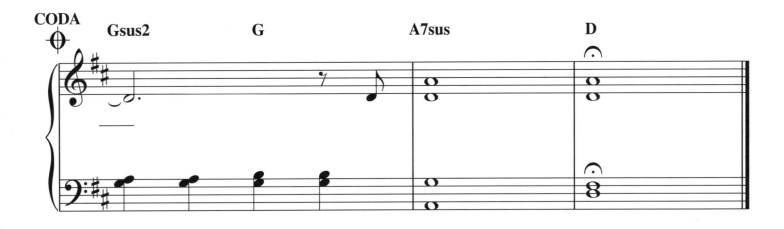

OPEN THE EYES OF MY HEART

Words and Music by
PAUL BALOCHE

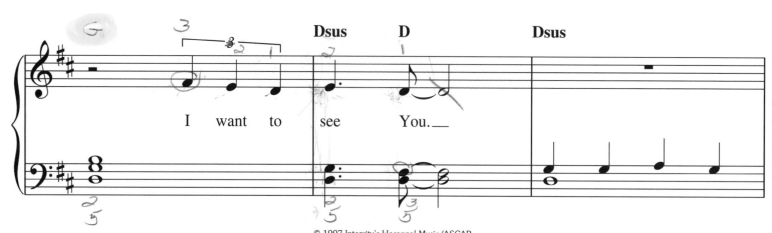

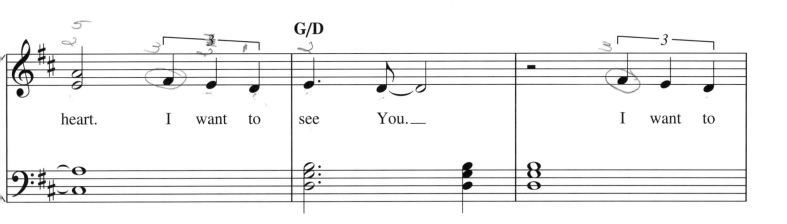

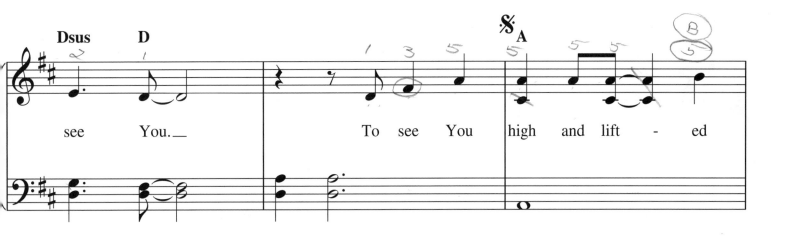

62

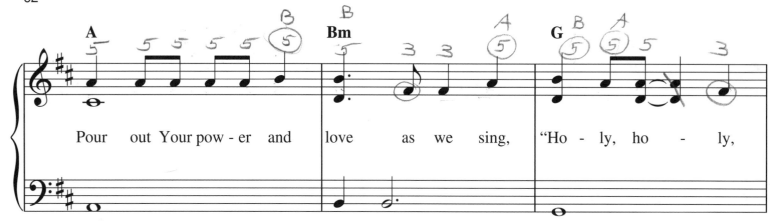

Pour out Your pow - er and love as we sing, "Ho - ly, ho - ly,

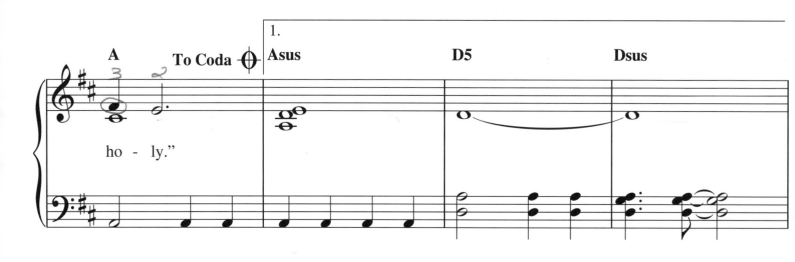

ho - ly."

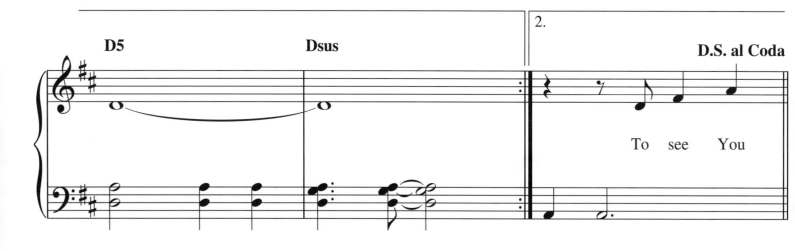

To see You

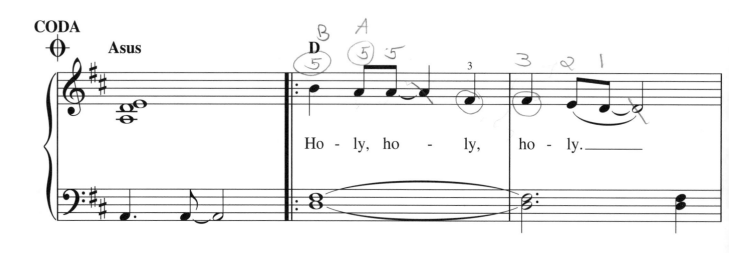

Ho - ly, ho - ly, ho - ly.

OUR LOVE IS LOUD

Words and Music by
DAVID CROWDER

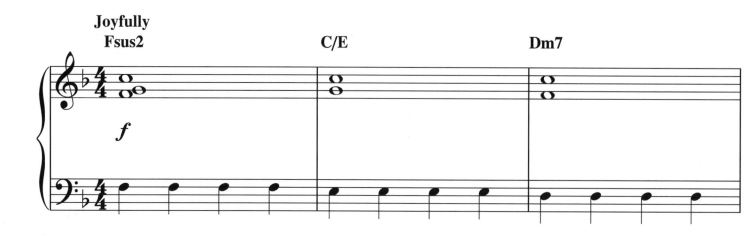

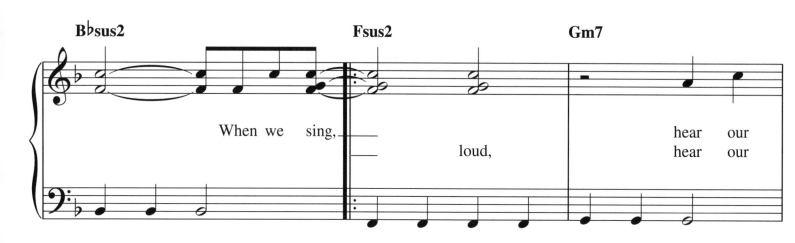

When we sing,_____ loud,

hear our
hear our

songs   to You._____   When we dance,_____
songs   to You._____   When we dance_____   'round,

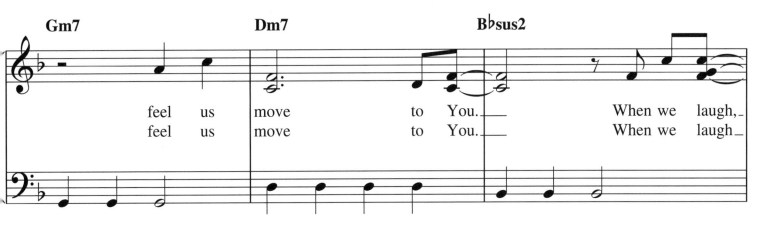

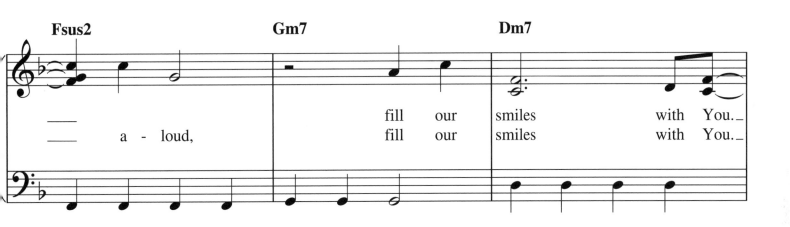

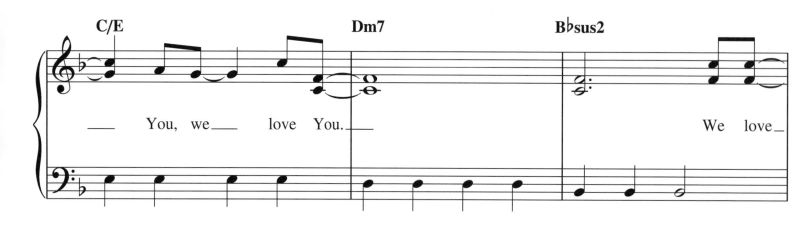

You, we love You. We love

You, Lord, we love You, we love You. **To Coda**

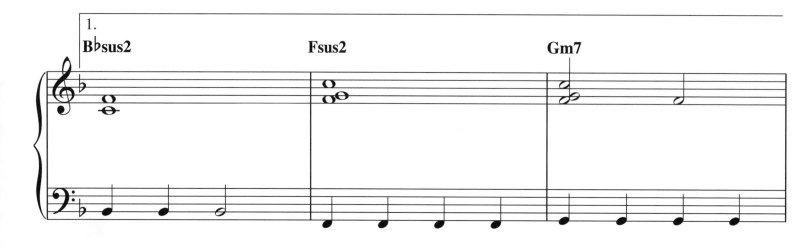

When we sing Our love

RAIN DOWN

Words and Music by MARTIN SMITH
and STUART GARRARD

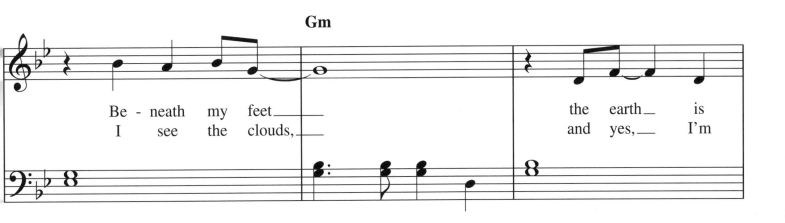

rain._____
hands._____

Yeah,_____ yeah._____
Yeah,_____ yeah._____

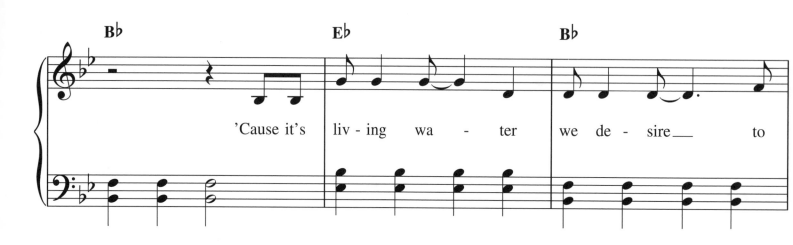

'Cause it's liv - ing wa - ter we de - sire_____ to

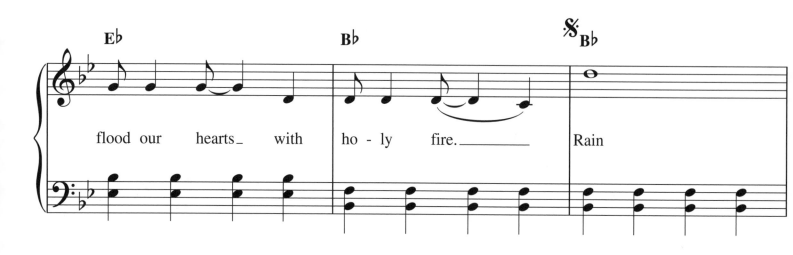

flood our hearts_ with ho - ly fire._____ Rain

down. All a - round_ the world_____ we're sing - ing.

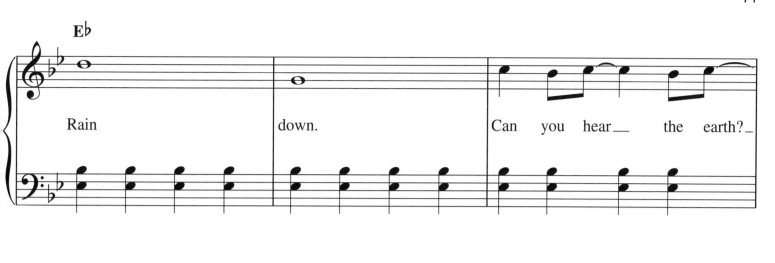

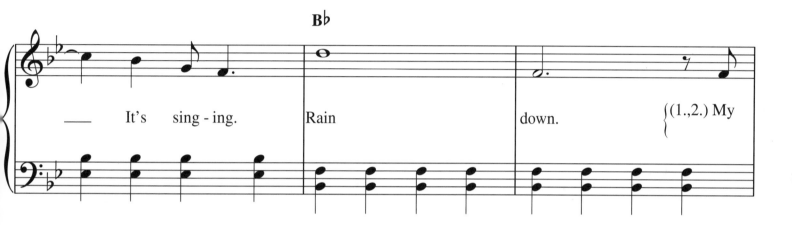

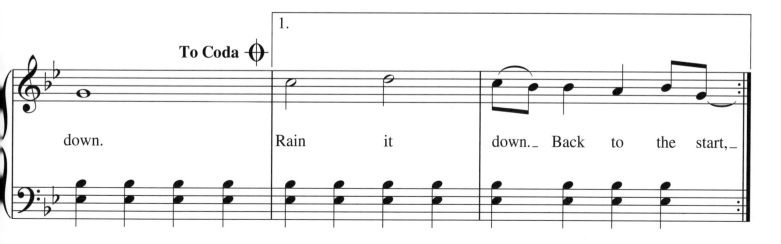

Rain it down. ____ Do not shut,

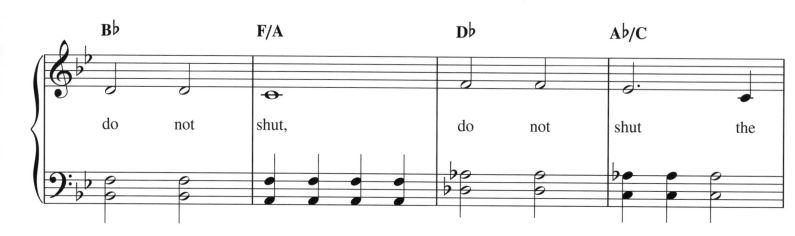

do not shut, do not shut the

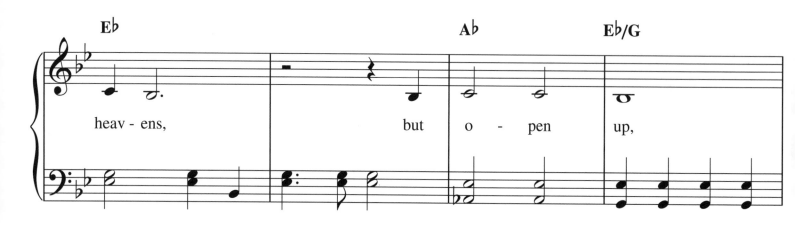

heav - ens, but o - pen up,

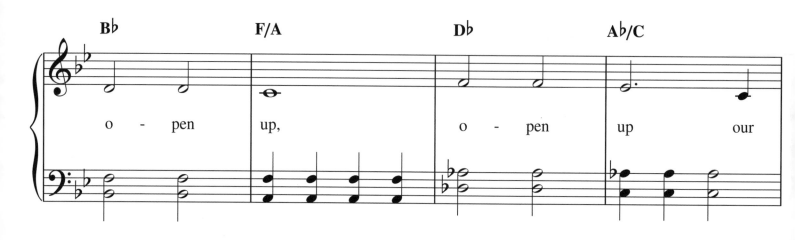

o - pen up, o - pen up our

SONG OF LOVE

Words and Music by REBECCA ST. JAMES,
MATT BRONLEEWE and JEREMY ASH

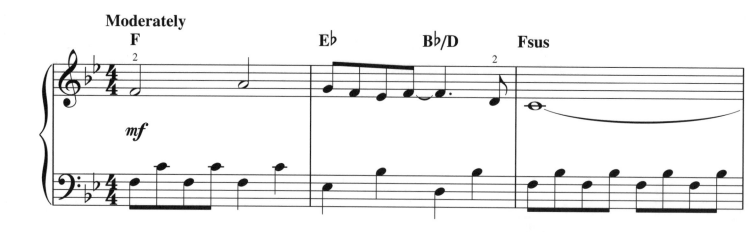

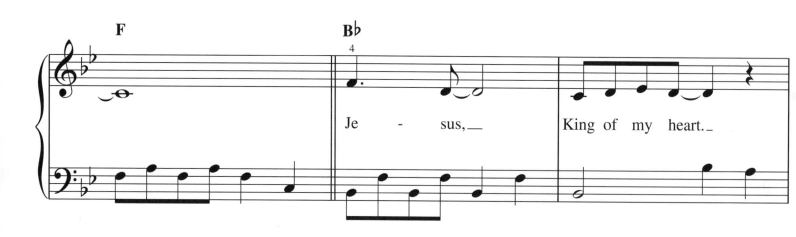

Je - sus,__ King of my heart.

Fa - ther,__ my peace and my light.__ Spir - it,___ the

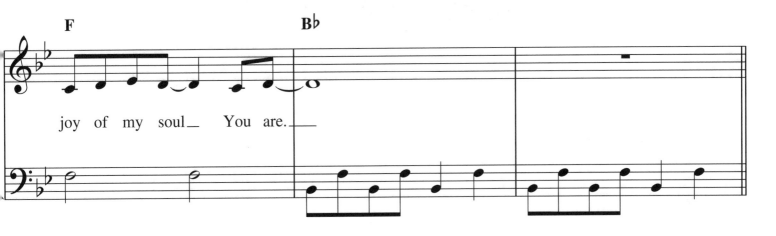

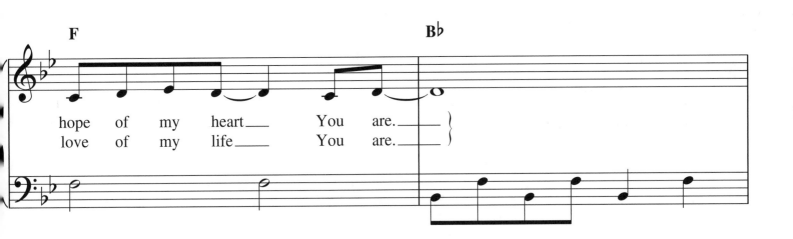

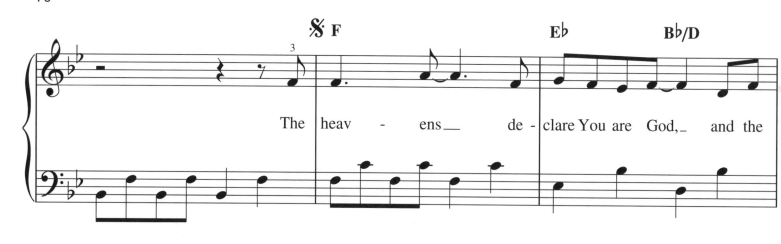

The heav - ens__ de - clare You are God,__ and the

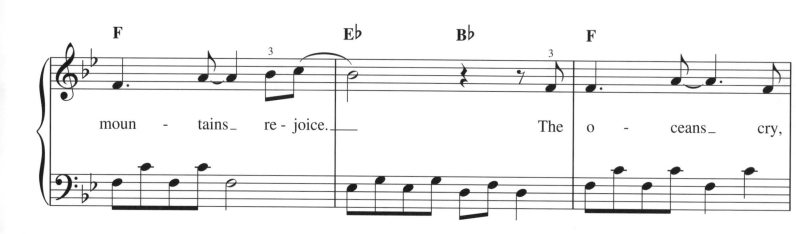

moun - tains__ re - joice.__ The o - ceans__ cry,

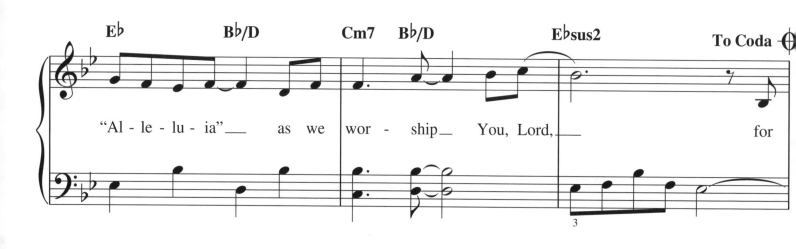

"Al - le - lu - ia"__ as we wor - ship__ You, Lord,__ for

this is our song__ of love.__

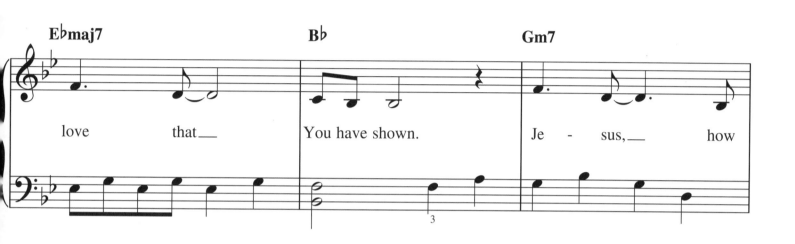

WE BOW DOWN

Words and Music by
TWILA PARIS

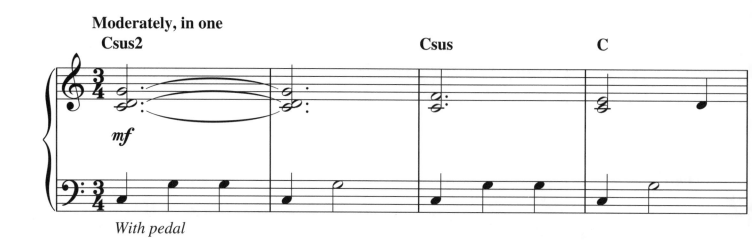

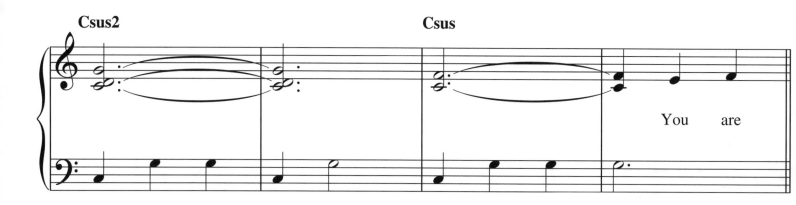

You are

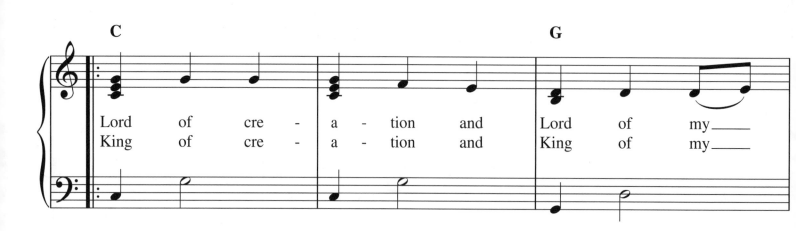

Lord of cre - a - tion and Lord of my___
King of cre - a - tion and King of my___

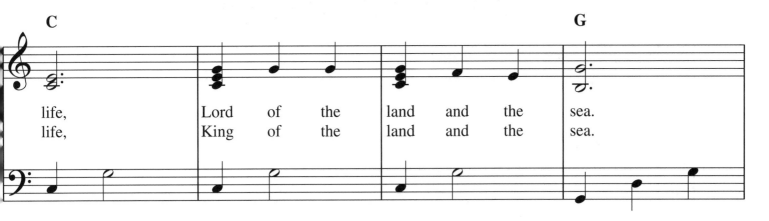

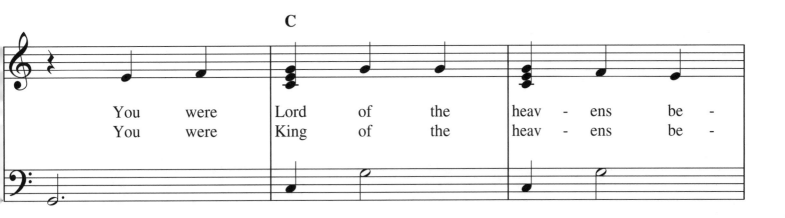

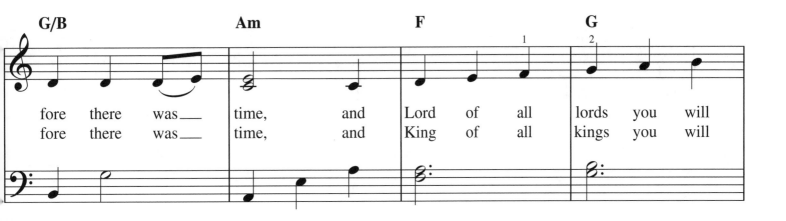

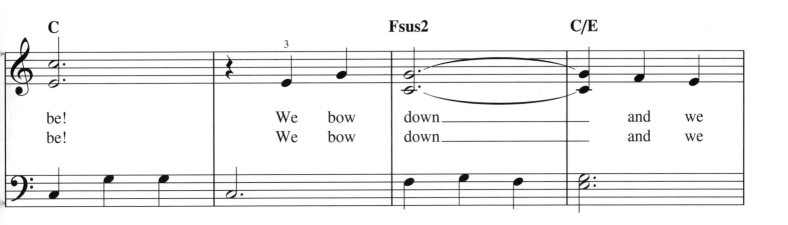

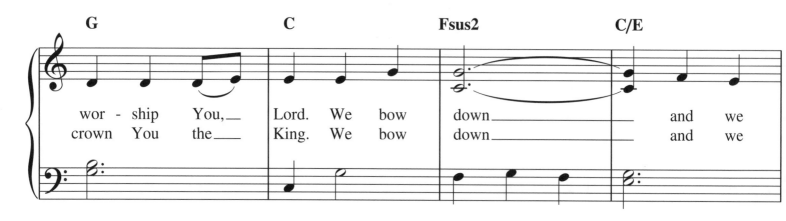

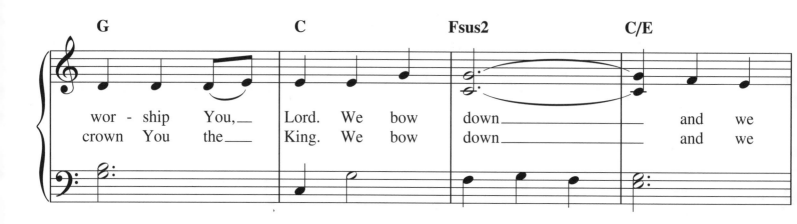

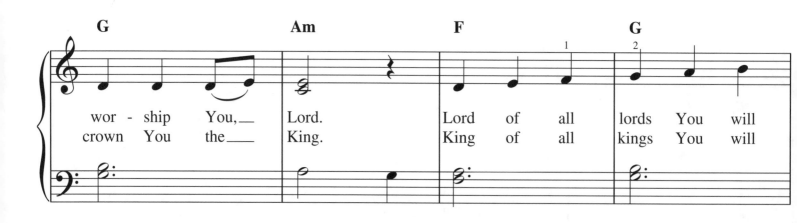

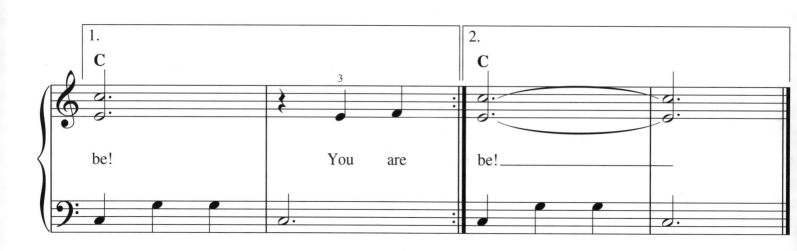

YOU ARE MY KING
(Amazing Love)

Words and Music by
BILLY JAMES FOOTE

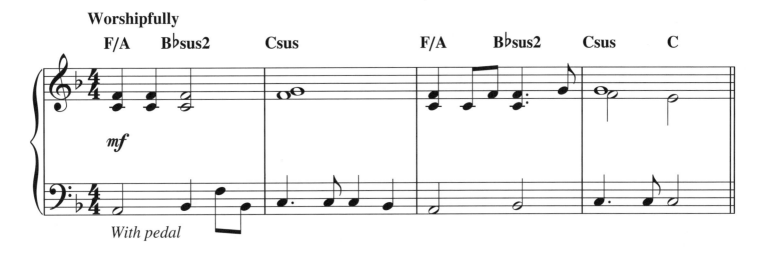

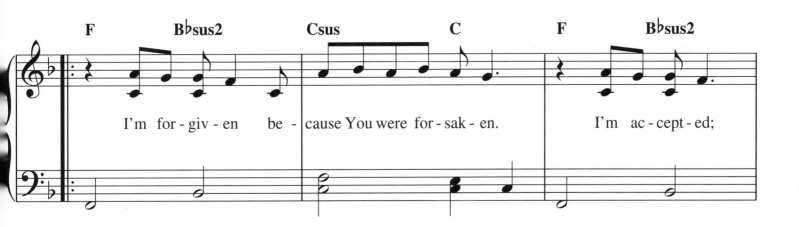

cause You died and rose a - gain.

A - maz-ing love, how—

— can it be—

that You, my King, would die for

me?

A - maz-ing love, I— know it's true;—

it's my joy to hon - or

You.

In all I do,—

I hon-or You.

1.

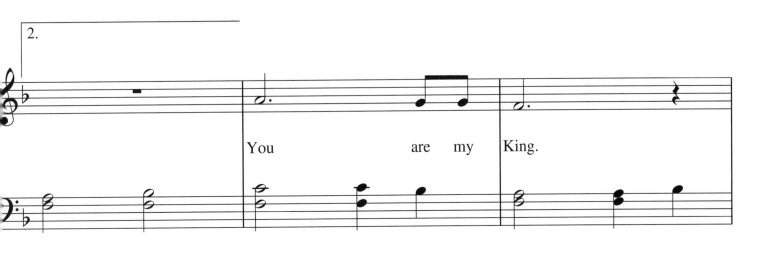

2.

You   are my King.

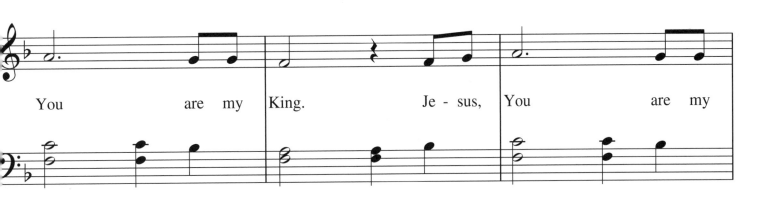

You   are my King.   Je - sus, You   are my

D.S. al Coda

King.   Je - sus, You   are my King.

CODA

B♭   C   F

do,_____   I   hon - or You.

WONDERFUL MAKER

Words and Music by CHRIS TOMLIN
and MATT REDMAN

C

You spread out Your arms
eye has ful - ly seen how

o - ver emp - ty hearts,
beau - ti - ful the cross, and

Em7

said, "Let there be light;"___ in - to a
we have on - ly heard___ the___

dark and hope - less world Your Son___
faint - est whis - pers of how great___

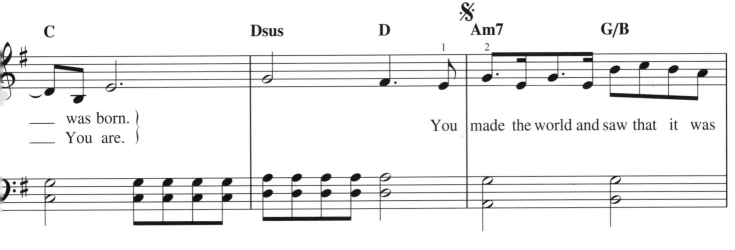

C   **Dsus**   **D**   **Am7**   **G/B**

___ was born.)
___ You are.)

You made the world and saw that it was

Csus2   **Am7**   **G/B**   **Csus2**

good.

You sent Your on - ly Son, for You are good.

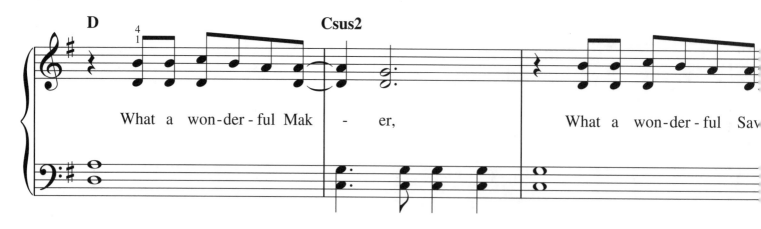

What a won-der-ful Mak - er, What a won-der-ful Sav

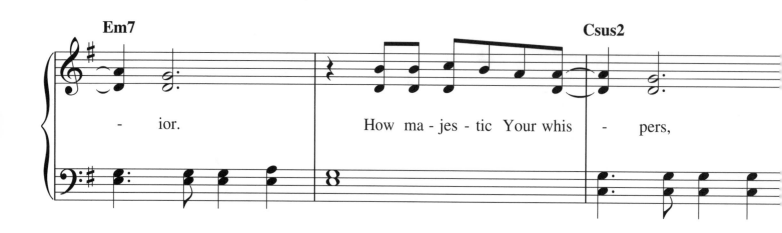

- ior. How ma - jes - tic Your whis - pers,

and how hum-ble Your love. With a strength like no oth

- er, and the heart of a Fa - ther,